Dedicated to my 2nd grade teacher,
Mrs. Brigid McGuire

Other books by Jayda Mayfield:
The World of Fairies
Thunder Twins-Vanessa vs. Melissa
Princess Zaree- Princess of Both Worlds

My Website: usbooklovers.com
YouTube: Jayda Tionne (Jayda's Journey)
Instagram: usbooklovers19
Facebook: Mayfield Jayda

Where is My Butterfly?

By Jayda Mayfield

Illustrated by Stacy Summerville

Edited by Fitzroy Thompson
Guest Editor: Beverly Bryan

ISBN: 9781722374938

Jayda Mayfield © 2018
All rights reserved

No parts of this book may be reproduced, stored, or transmitted in any form or by any means, electronic, mechanical, or photocopying, or otherwise, without prior written permission of the author, except as provided by USA copyright law.

On a hot day in the town of Fredrick, a butterfly named Mel had an egg on a leaf in a beautiful garden. The garden belonged to a young girl named Claire. She was six years old and did not know much about butterflies. Claire was excited because she was starting kindergarten in a few weeks.

One day, Claire went to play in her garden and found Mel's egg. She asked her mom what it was and she told her it was a butterfly's egg. Claire's mom decided to search the internet to find out more about butterfly eggs. They learned that the egg was a Monarch butterfly. Claire invited her best friends Rosa and Clarissa to see the egg.

When Rosa and Clarissa arrived, they all rushed to the garden to see the egg.

Suddenly, Claire yelled, "**Where is my egg?**"

All that was there was a yellow and black worm.

Claire's mom searched the internet to find out more about the worm.

Suddenly, everyone yelled, "Ohhhhhhh, it's a caterpillar!"

They learned that in a week or two, a butterfly's egg hatches into a caterpillar.

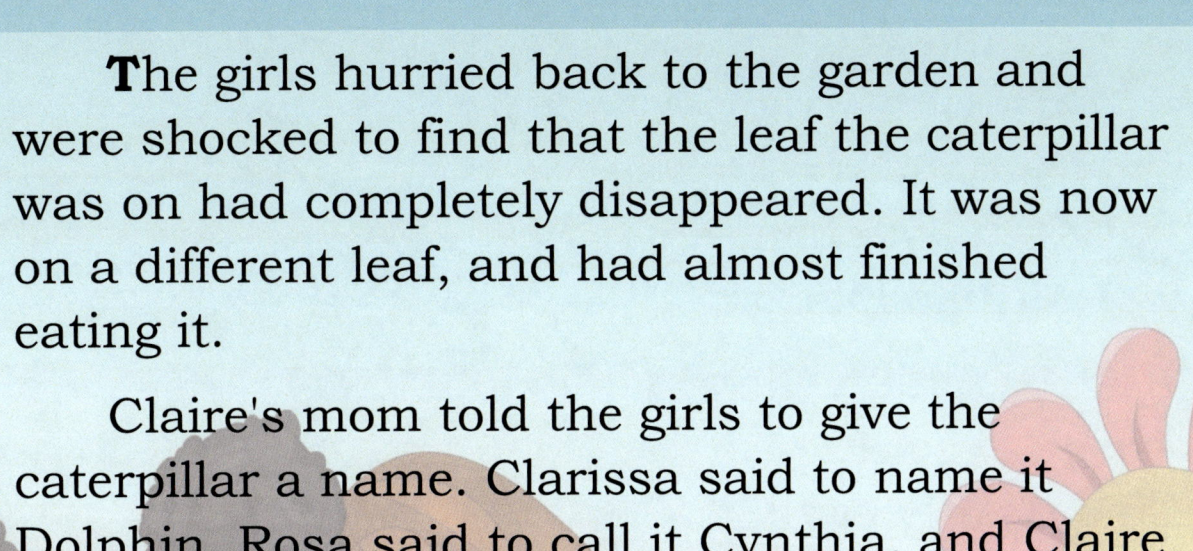

The girls hurried back to the garden and were shocked to find that the leaf the caterpillar was on had completely disappeared. It was now on a different leaf, and had almost finished eating it.

Claire's mom told the girls to give the caterpillar a name. Clarissa said to name it Dolphin, Rosa said to call it Cynthia, and Claire said, "**Melva**, I shall name it **Melva**."

Claire placed Melva into a cup and decided to give her a tour of Fredrick Street. They showed Melva the park, the shopping center, and the Library.

At the Library, the girls read books about caterpillars. They still didn't know that Melva would soon turn into a chrysalis.

They stopped by the ocean to watch the sunset.

After a few minutes of watching the sunset, they noticed that Melva had fallen asleep so they decided that it was time to head home.

When Claire got home, she placed Melva on a new leaf in the garden.

The next morning, Claire went to check on Melva.

Suddenly, she shouted, "**Where Is My Caterpillar**?"

All that was there was an oval-shaped pod. She asked her mom what it was. Her mom was not sure what it was so she read one of the books they got from the Library.

They learned that caterpillars create a home called chrysalis and that the chrysalis needs sunlight to transform into a butterfly. This process is called metamorphosis. They also learned that butterflies eat garden food and plants such as, milkweed, nectar, parsley, fennel, dill, and carrots. Claire was excited to learn that the butterfly will take two weeks or more to come out of the chrysalis.

Two weeks later, Claire, Rosa, and Clarissa were starting Kindergarten. Claire was no longer excited to start school because she wanted to see her butterfly come out of the chrysalis.

Claire's mom promised her that the butterfly would not fly away until she got home from school. She explained that it takes a couple of hours for the wings to dry up before a butterfly is able to fly for the first time. Claire was relieved to hear that.

On the first day of school, Claire learned about monarch butterflies.

When she got home, Claire ran to the garden. Neither the butterfly nor the chrysalis was there. She ran to her mom with tears in her eyes.

"**Where is my butterfly**? "Claire cried.

She hugged her mom, and she felt something behind her back. It was a jar.

Claire took the jar from her mom's hands. Inside the jar, there was a beautiful monarch butterfly. She laughed, she jumped, and she was happy.

Claire invited her friends over to see her monarch butterfly.

They were amazed by its beautiful colors. The colors were reddish-orange with black markings and a few white spots.

The next day at school, they went on a field trip to a butterfly garden. The garden was beautiful; there were pink, red, and blue flowers.

They went inside a little building full of butterflies. They saw many different types of butterflies. There were more colors than a rainbow. They were overjoyed.

The owner of the garden told them interesting facts about butterflies. He also told them that they could make their own butterfly garden, using plants that attract butterflies. That was great news for Claire. She had the biggest smile ever because it amazed her to learn that she could have hundreds of butterflies in her backyard.

After school, Claire and her mom went to the store and bought seeds for flowers that would attract butterflies. They planted the seeds everywhere. A few months later, the seeds grew into beautiful flowers, and there were butterflies everywhere.

THE END

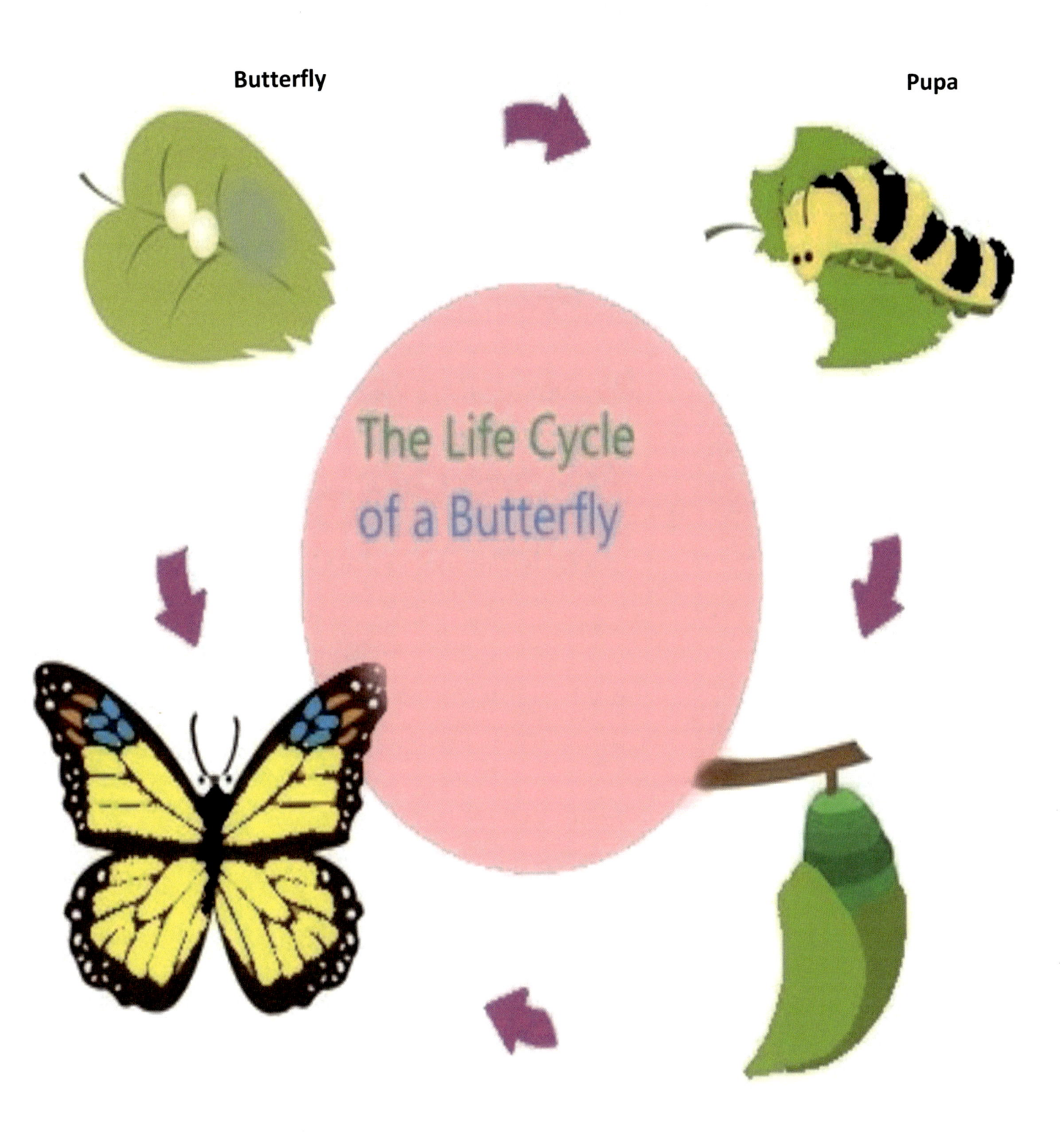

Butterfly **Pupa**

The Life Cycle of a Butterfly

About the Author

My name is Jayda Mayfield, and I am ten years old. I wrote this book when I was in second grade, after learning about the life cycle of butterflies. I started writing stories when I was about four years old. I love reading and writing. Whenever I learn something interesting in school, I go home and write a story about it using my imagination. I hope that this book will inspire other kids to read and write using their own imagination.

If you enjoyed this book please let me know by leaving a review on Amazon. Thanks!

Made in the USA
Middletown, DE
07 August 2021

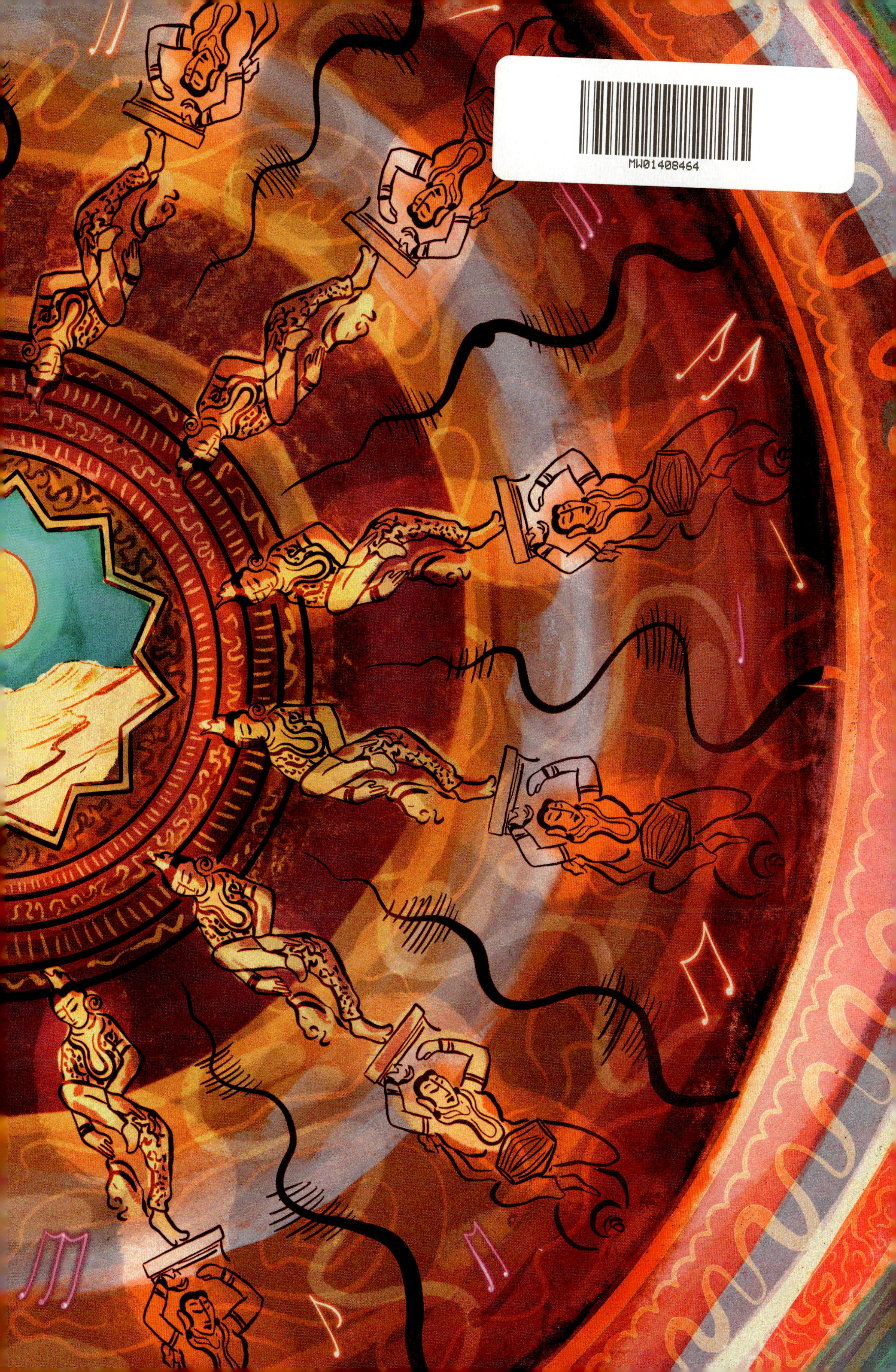

To those who dare. Not softly. Not quietly.
Thank you for your inspiration.
—J.R.G.

To all the queers who have held me
through storms and spring.
—S.K.

This is an Arthur A. Levine book
Published by Levine Querido

LQ
LEVINE QUERIDO

Levine Querido
www.levinequerido.com • info@levinequerido.com

Levine Querido is distributed by Chronicle Books, LLC.

Text copyright © 2023 by Jyoti Rajan Gopal
Illustration copyright © 2023 by Svabhu Kohli

All rights reserved
Library of Congress Control Number: 2023931660
ISBN 9781646142620

Printed in China

MIX
Paper | Supporting
responsible forestry
FSC™ C104723

Published October 2023
First Printing

The text type was set in Brandon Text.

DESERT QUEEN

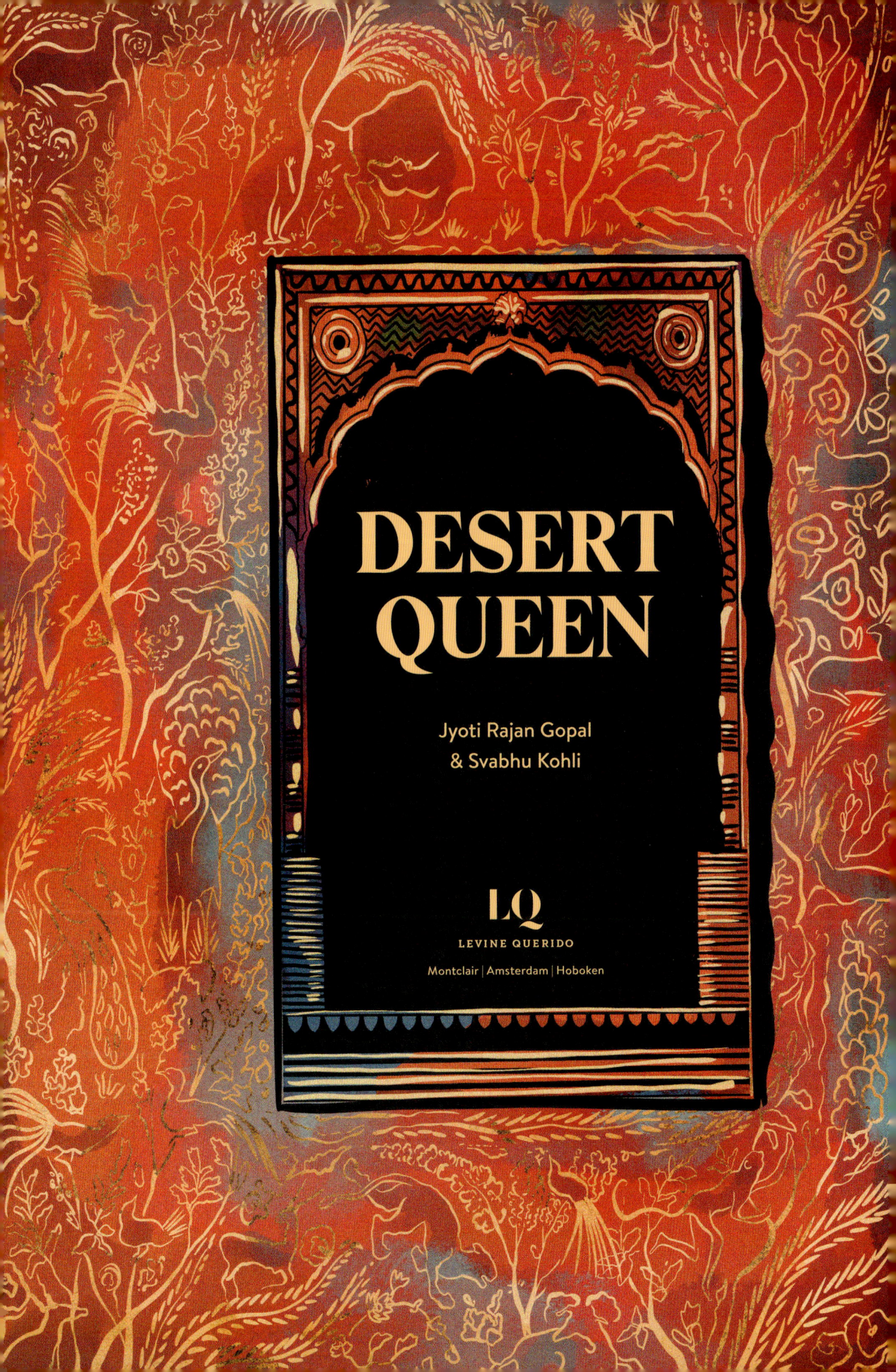

Jyoti Rajan Gopal
& Svabhu Kohli

LQ

LEVINE QUERIDO

Montclair | Amsterdam | Hoboken

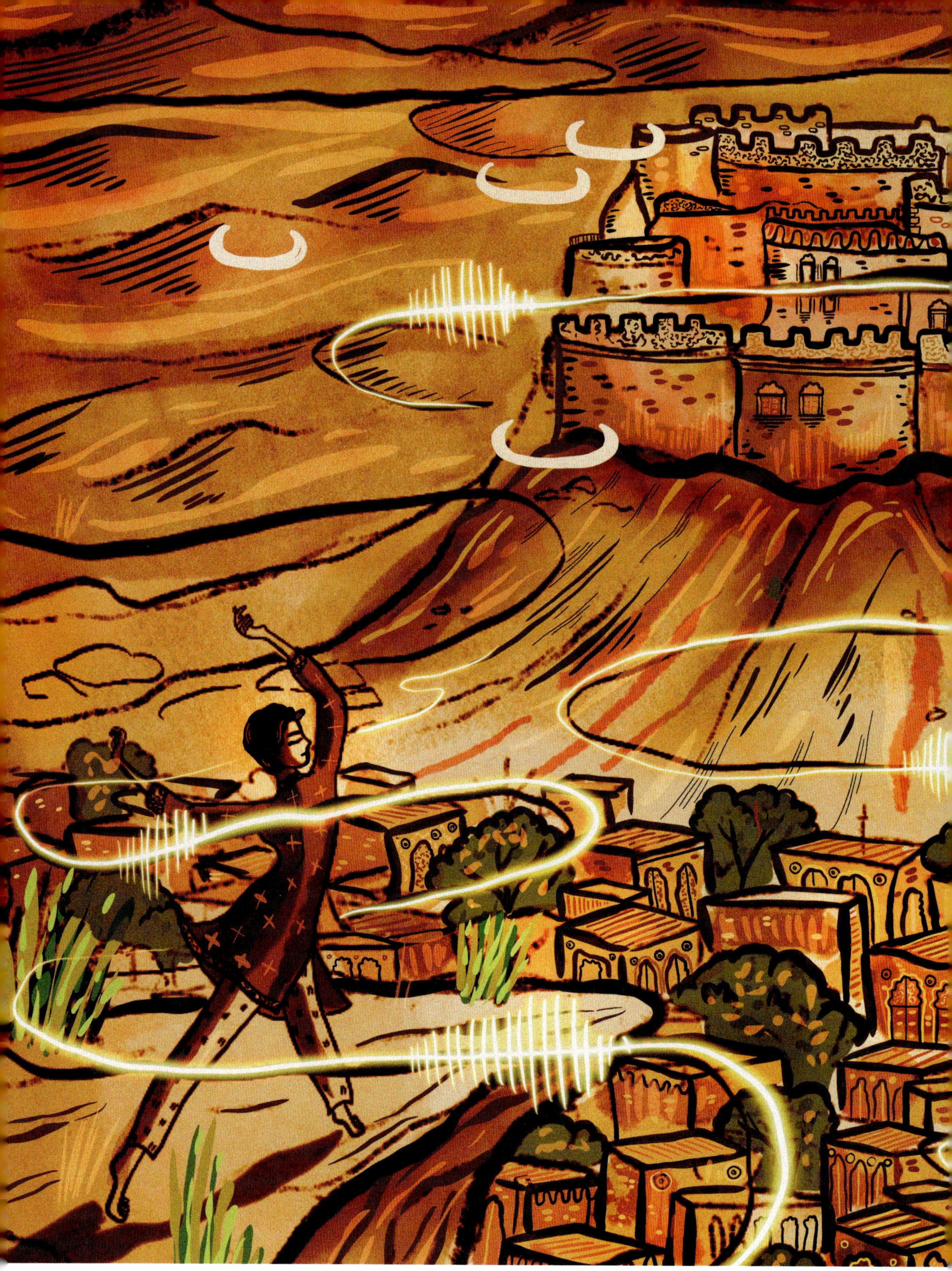

There is a boy...
who lives in the Thar Desert.

Thumris and *ragas* soar in his mind.
Rhythms pulse through his body.
The music sings clarion clear in his heart.

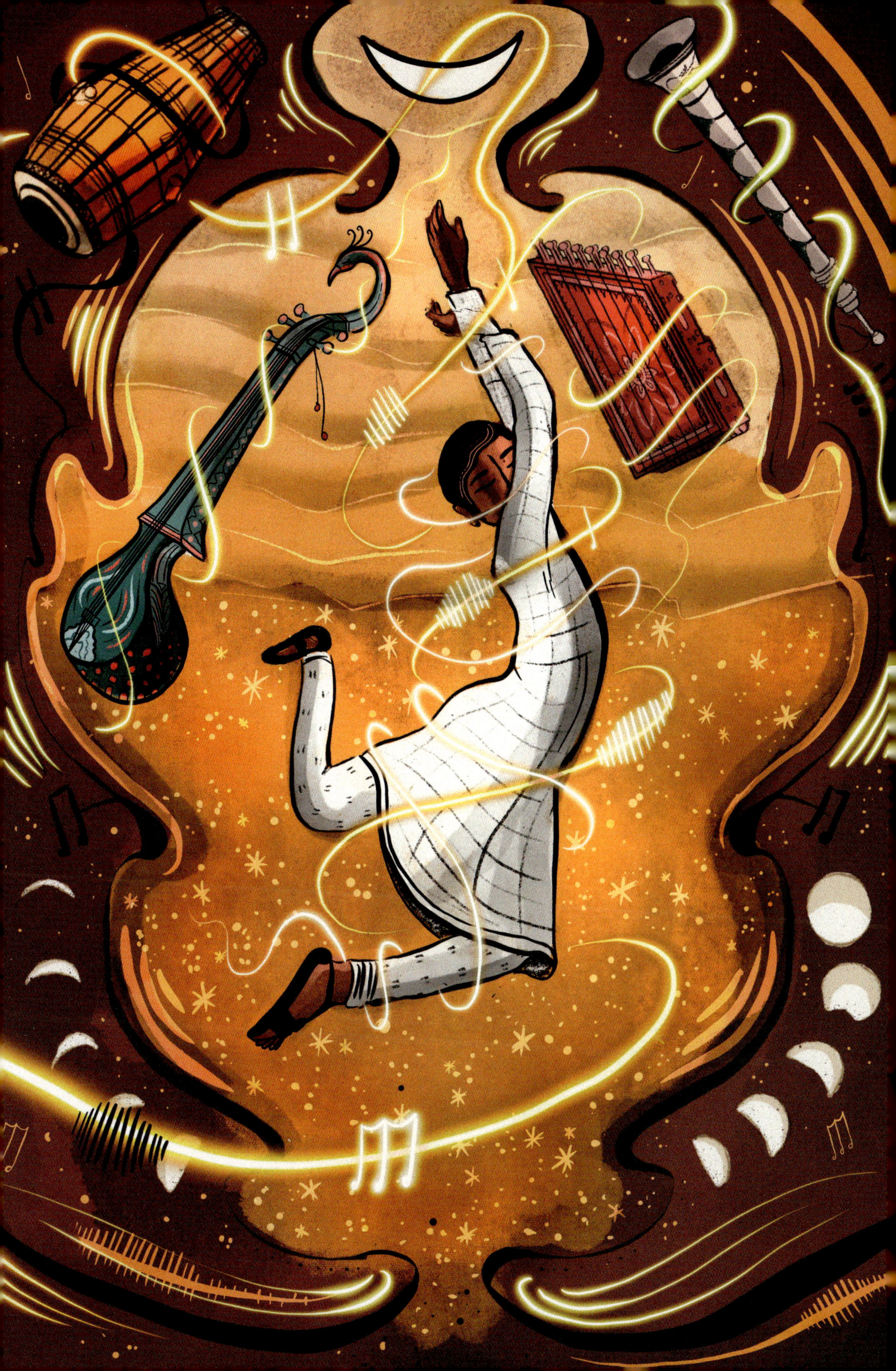

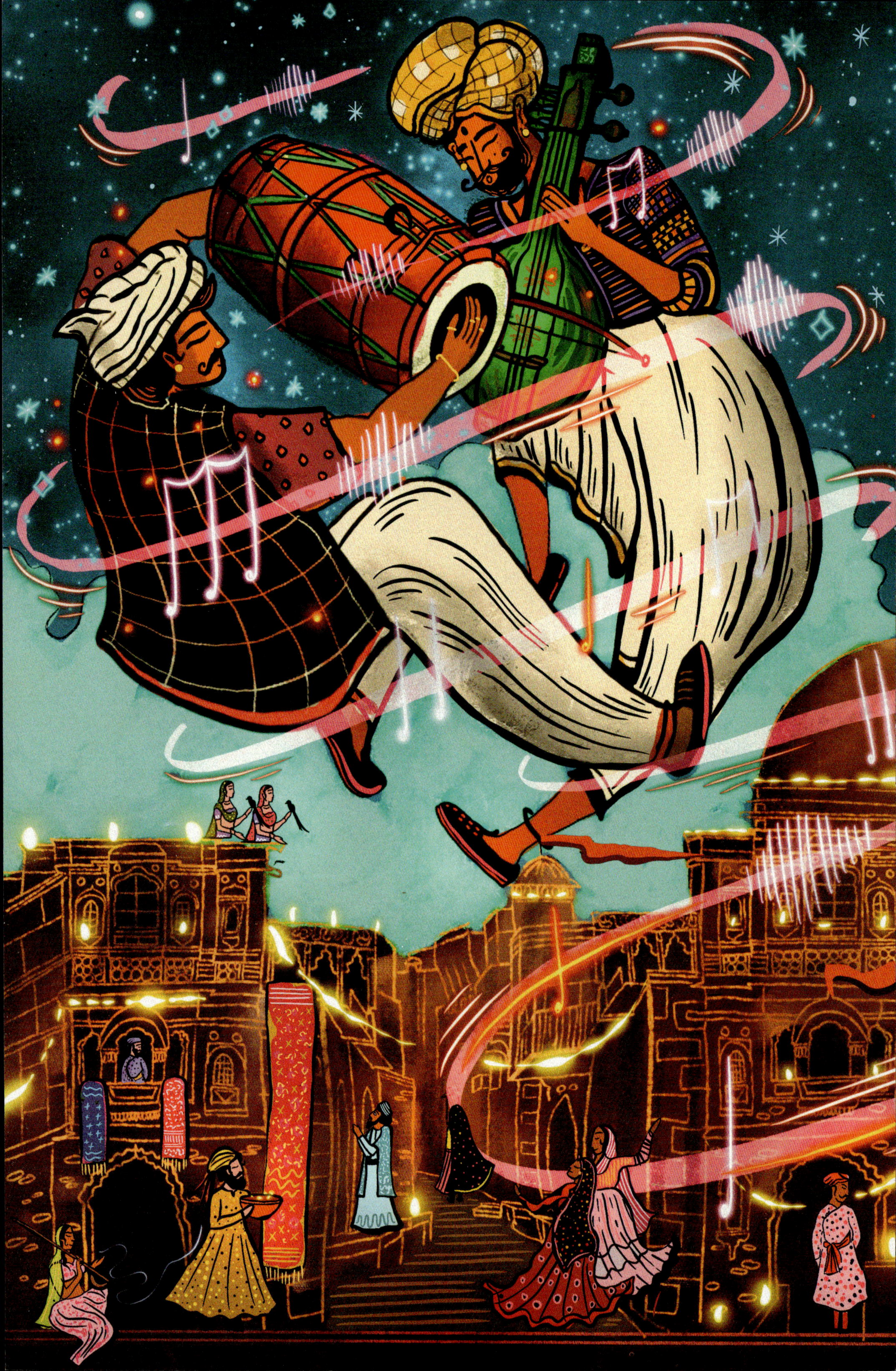

And yet... yet...
When the *khamaicha* thrums
and the *dholak* drums
and the boy's feet tap
and his fingers sway...
it is softly... softly, so no one sees.

When images dance across the screen
to a beat that shimmers and bounces,
spins and turns unfold in his mind,
step by step,
but quietly... quietly, so no one sees.

In his desert world,
there are lines in the sand
that keep you in your place.
Boy OR girl.
Man OR woman.
The boy knows this.

Then one day, at school,
a door cracks open.
A chance to be
another.

The boy becomes
Lord Krishna.
He, of black-rimmed eyes
and mischievous smiles,
of flowing fabric
and dazzling jewels.

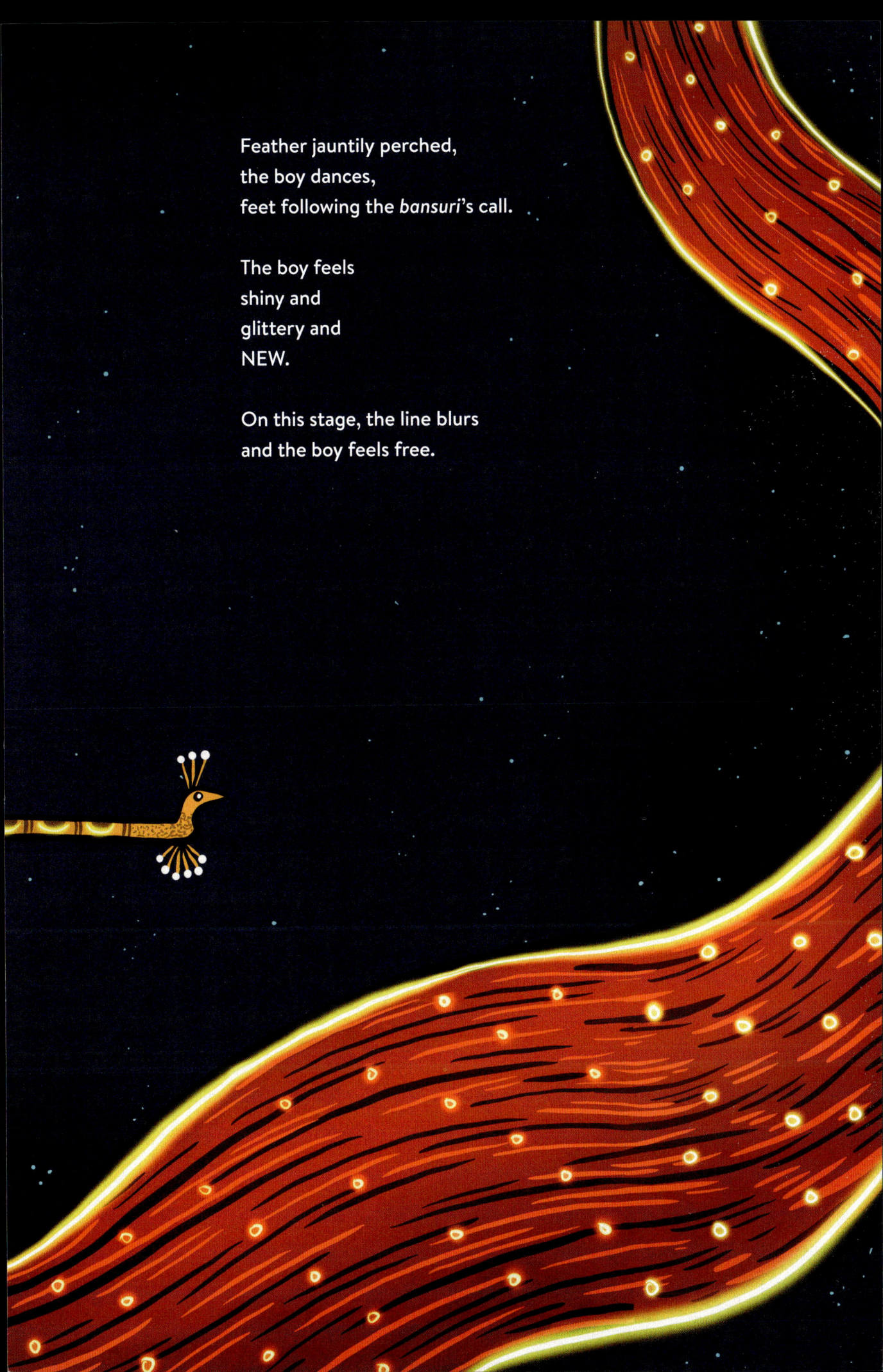

Feather jauntily perched,
the boy dances,
feet following the *bansuri*'s call.

The boy feels
shiny and
glittery and
NEW.

On this stage, the line blurs
and the boy feels free.

Unexpectedly, the boy's world shifts.
A deep rift opens.
Mother gone, a sickness wasting her away.
Father gone soon after, crushed by grief.

The boy is alone.

Alone with two sisters
to care for.
He aches with loss...
and worry.

Worry for his sisters.
Worry for his home.
How will they live?
Who will take care of them?

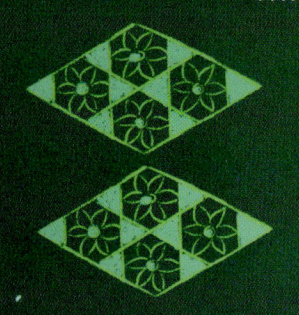

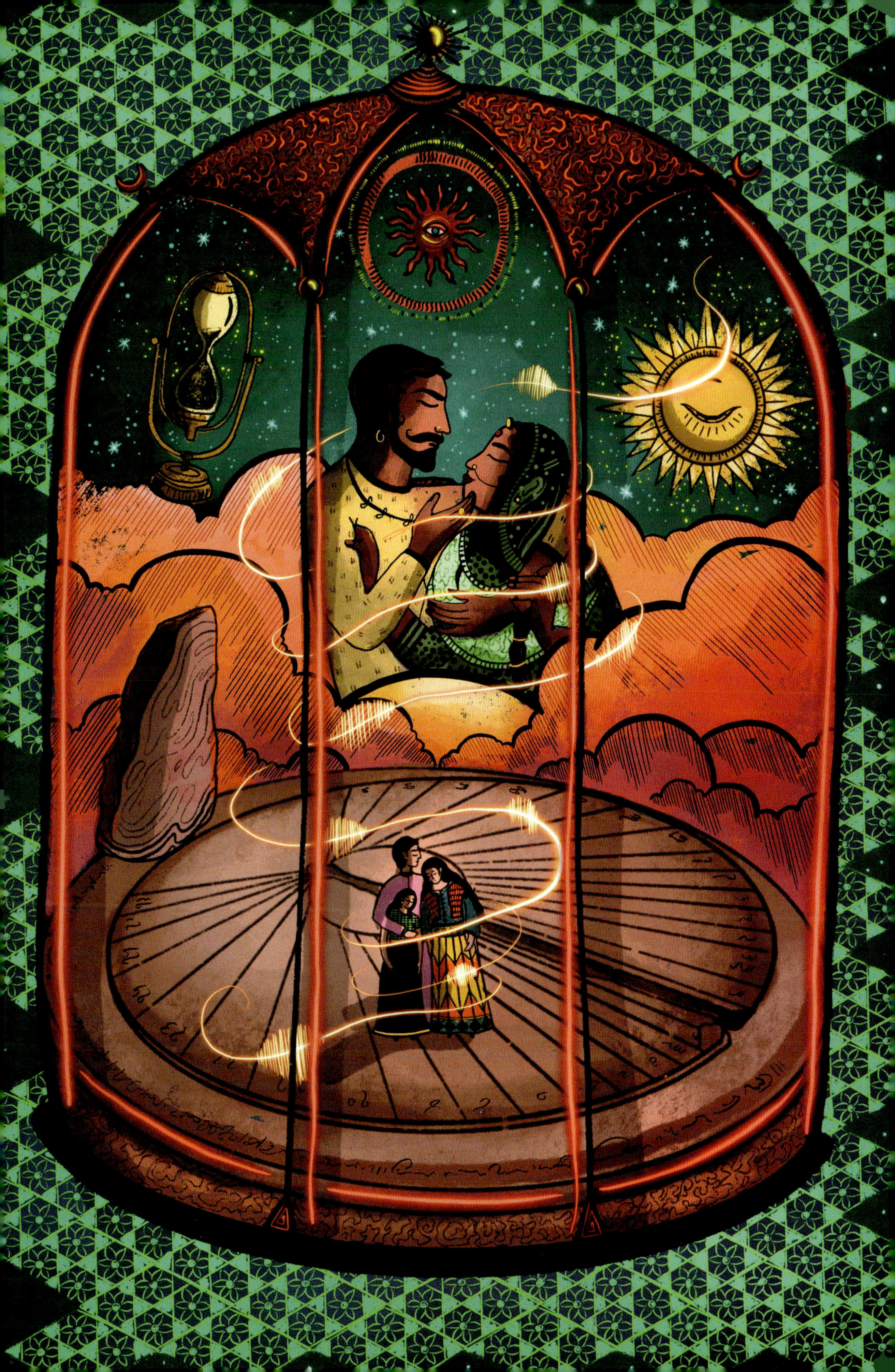

Then...
a hint
a glint.

Krishna beckons,
luminous in his silks
and jewels.
He of the beguiling smile
and the dancing eyes.

The boy has a thought,
an idea – a BOLD idea.

He wonders.
Can he?
Dare he?

A *ghagra*, mirrored and flowing.
A *choli*, brightly patterned.
Kajol-lined eyes.
Bright red lipstick.

Ghunghroo-clad ankles
and bangles that sparkle.

The boy is shiny and glittery and NEW.

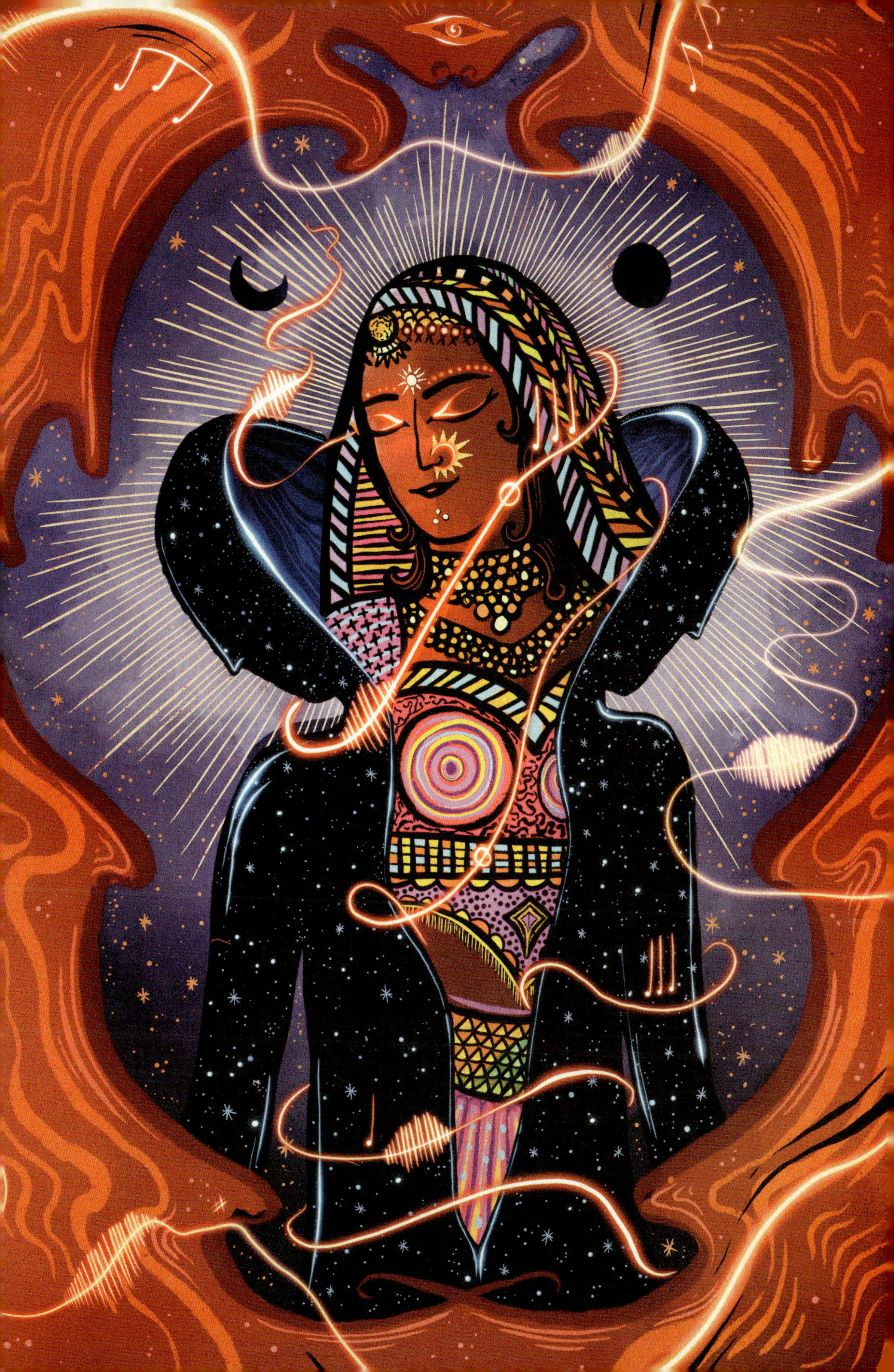

He slips into the dance,
heart thumping,
feet tapping.

Dip,
sway,
spin.

Spin,
sway,
dip.

Again
and again...
and again.

Ghagra,
whirling, twirling,
a kaleidoscope of
dancing, dancing...
DANCING.

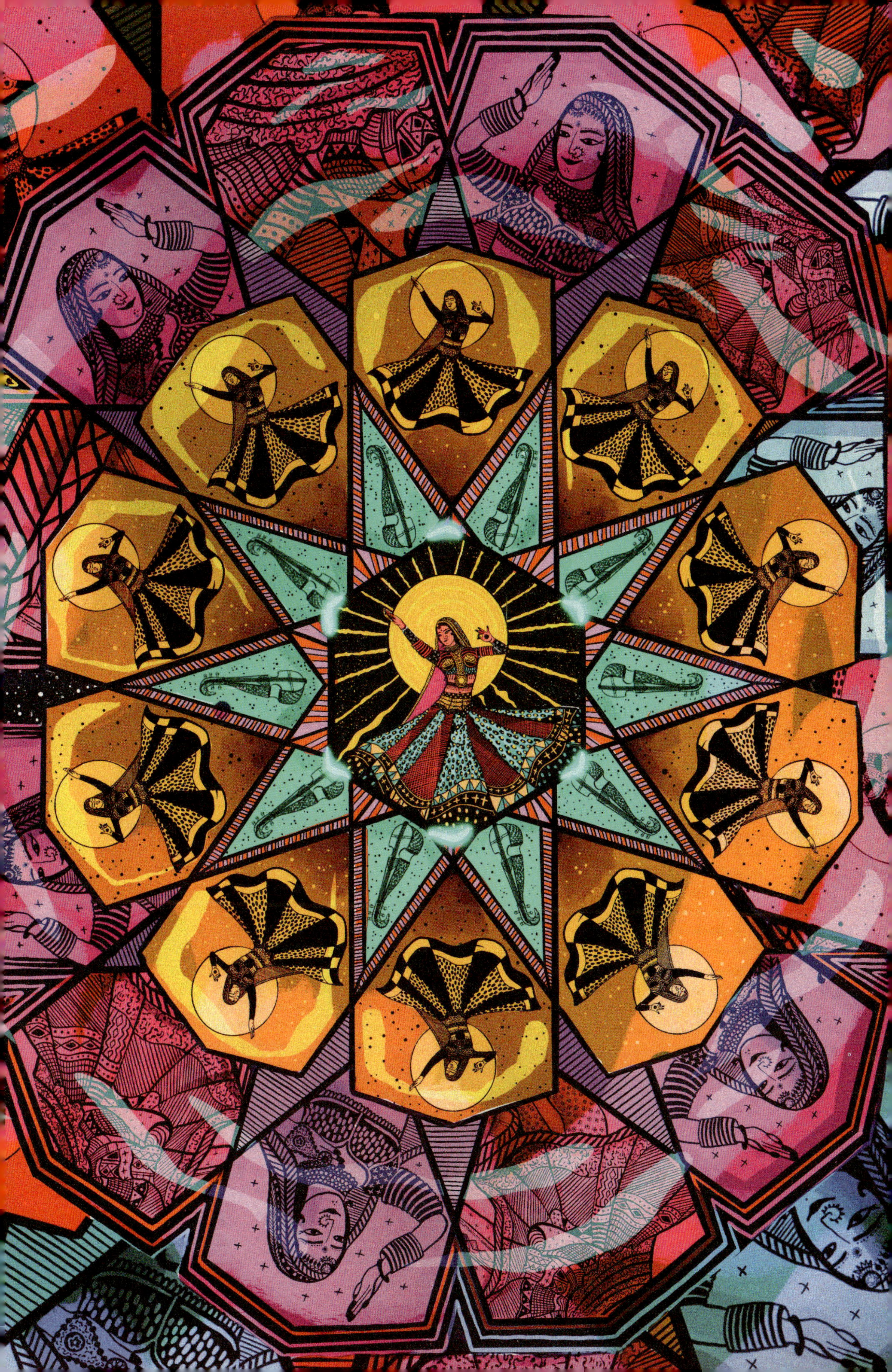

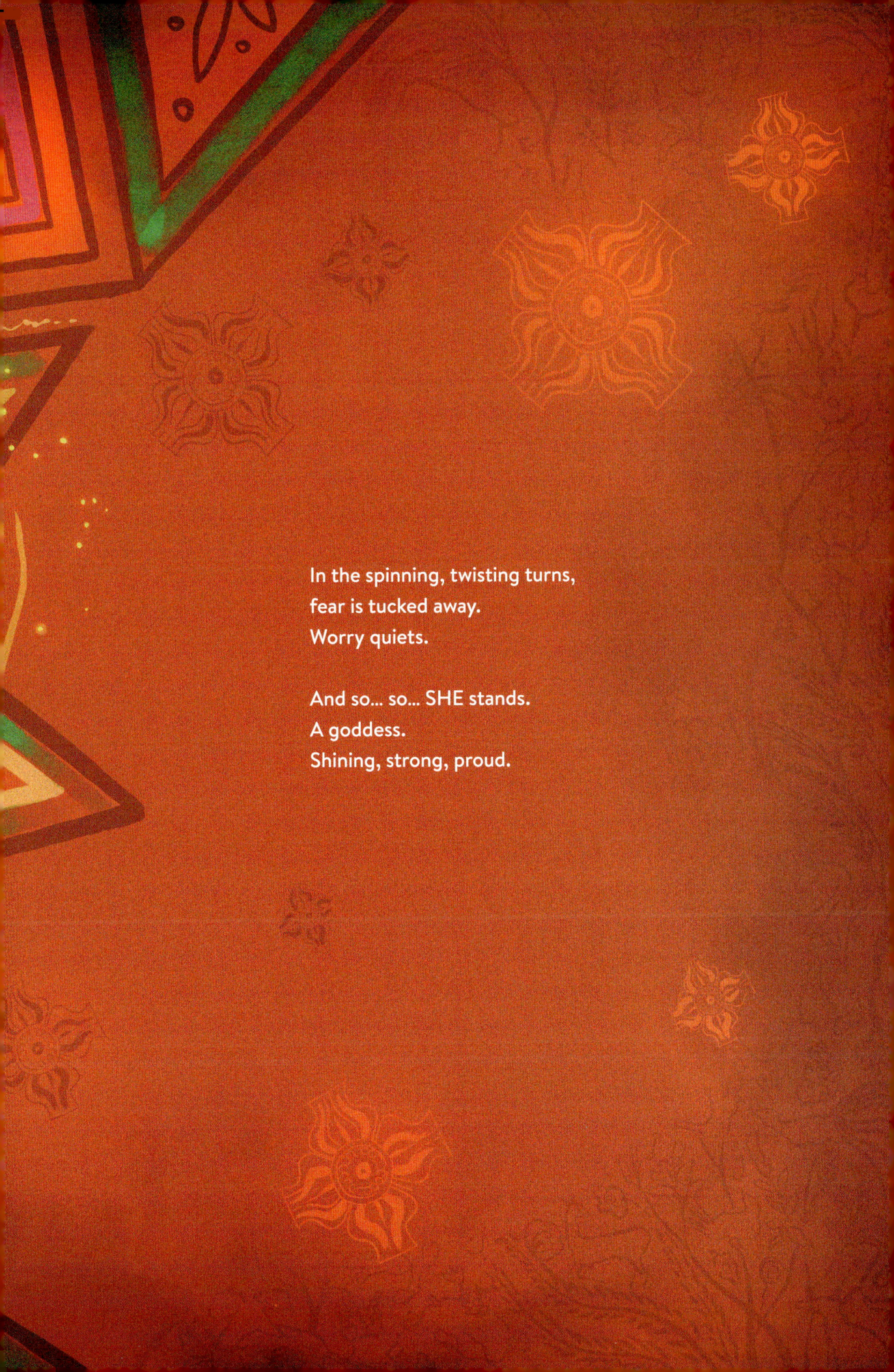

In the spinning, twisting turns,
fear is tucked away.
Worry quiets.

And so... so... SHE stands.
A goddess.
Shining, strong, proud.

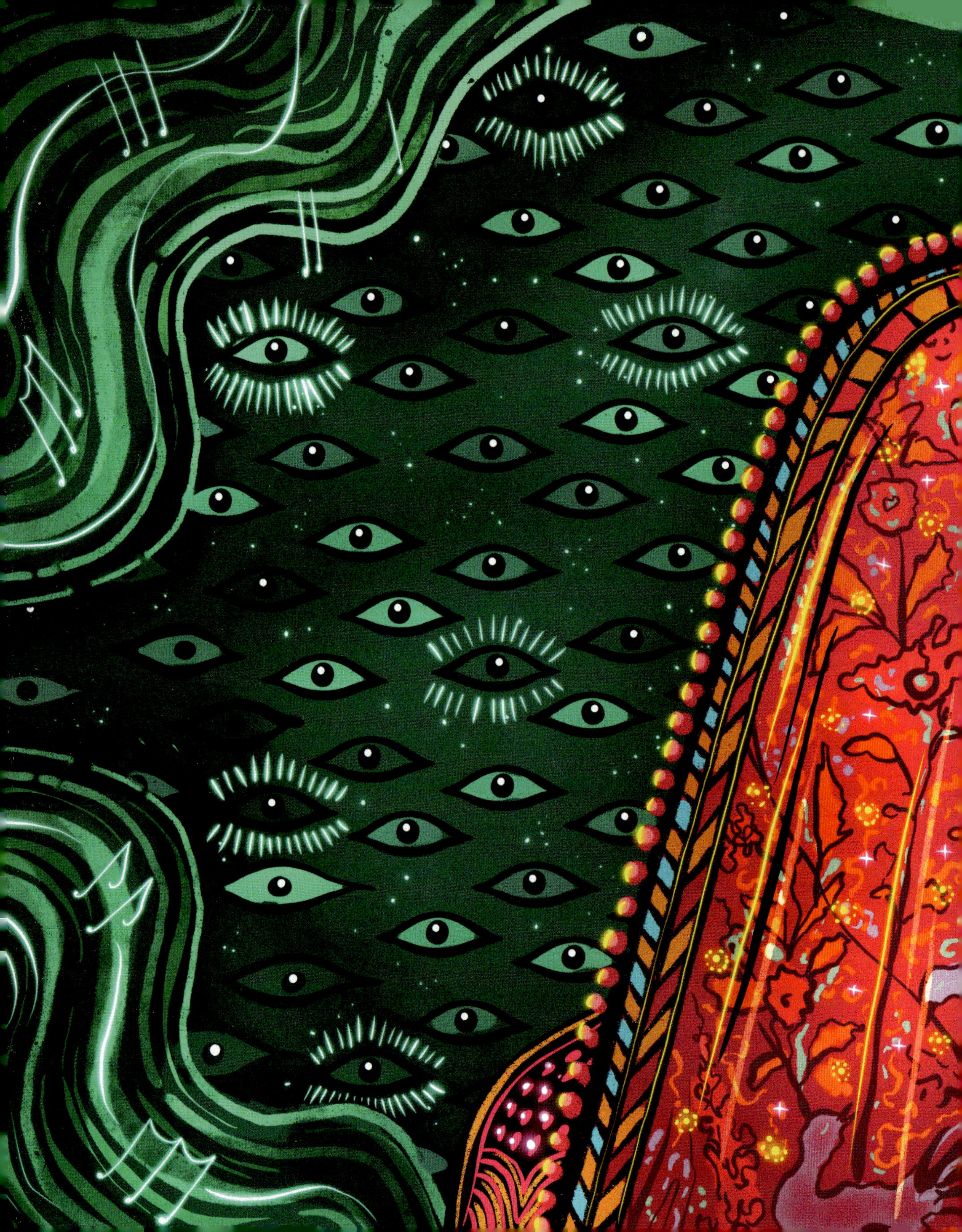

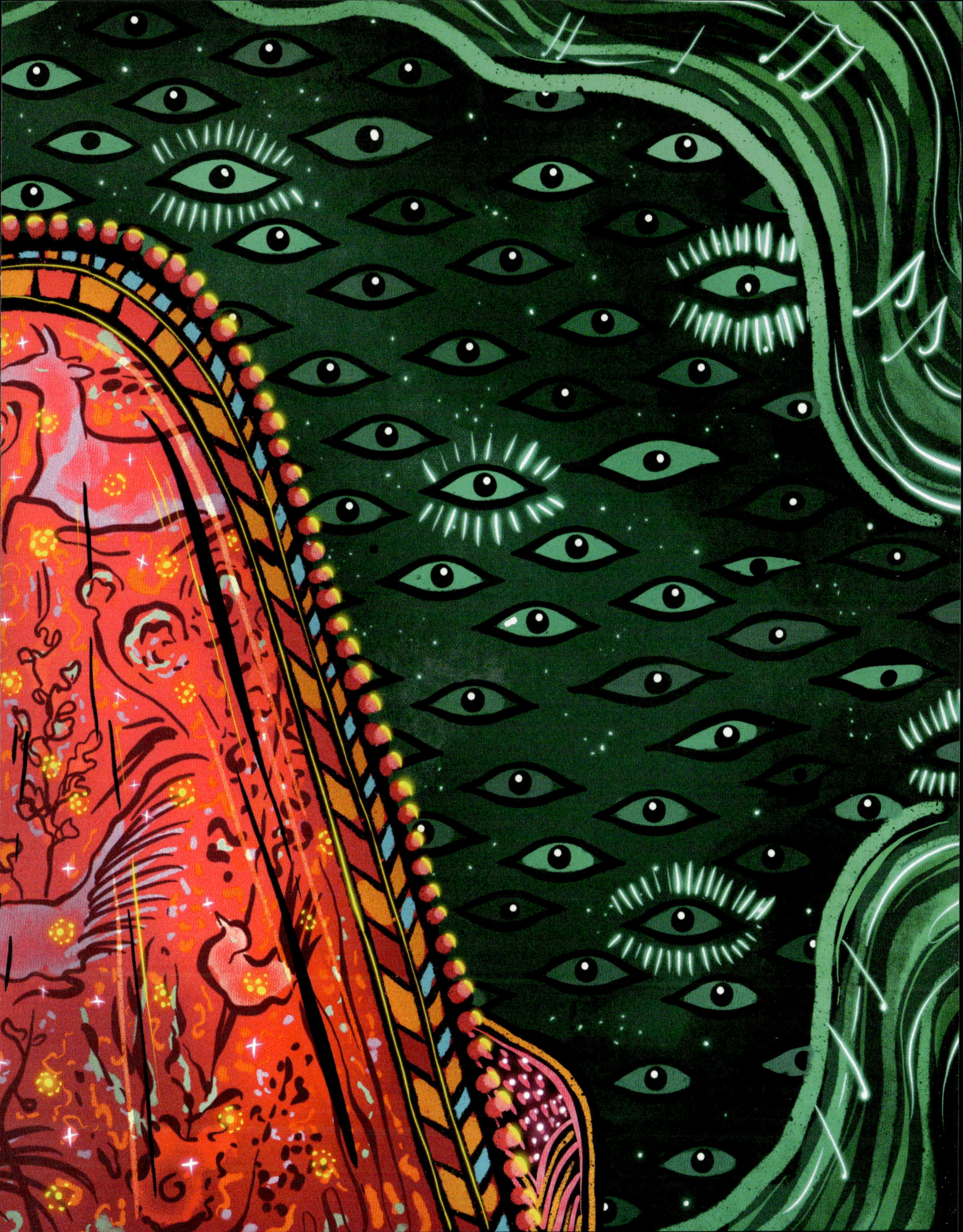

and her heart
fills with peace.
She knows... KNOWS
that this is where she belongs.

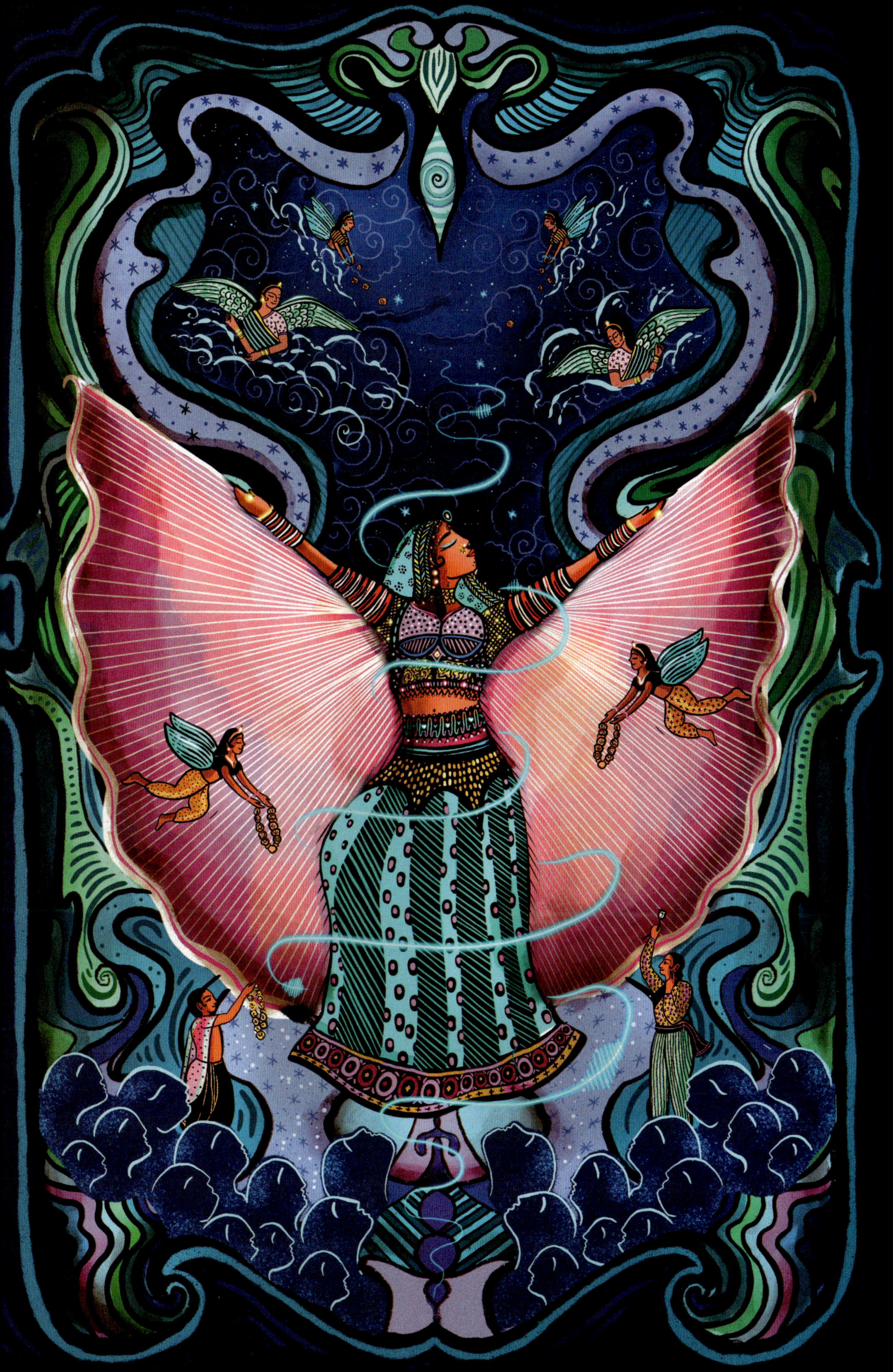

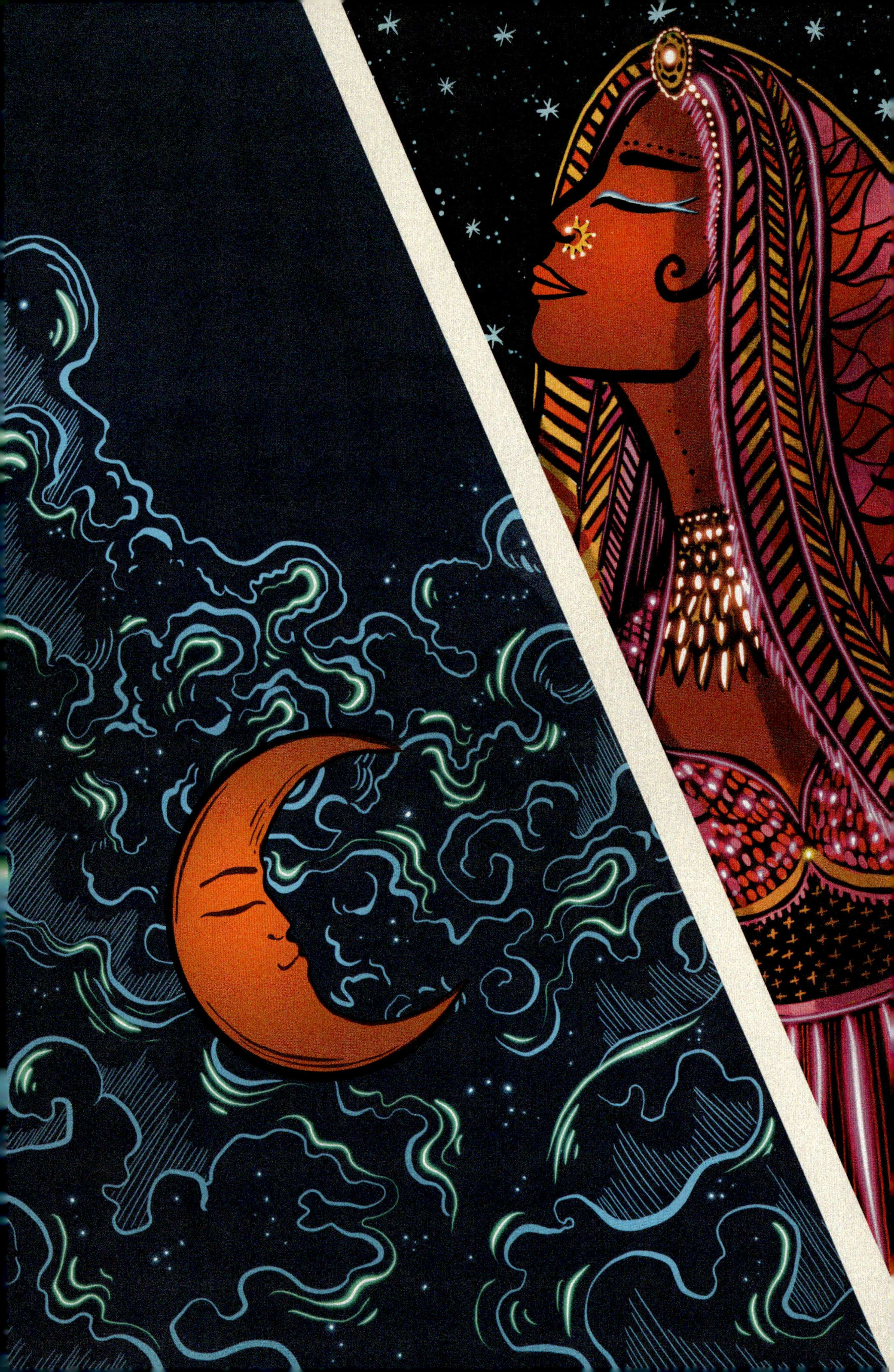

Daybreak.
The girl slips back into boy,
and her world flips.

Harsh,
cruel,
ugly words
are thrown at him
like stones.
Taunts that pierce and jab.

The boy flinches.
Afraid.
Ashamed.
And yet... yet...

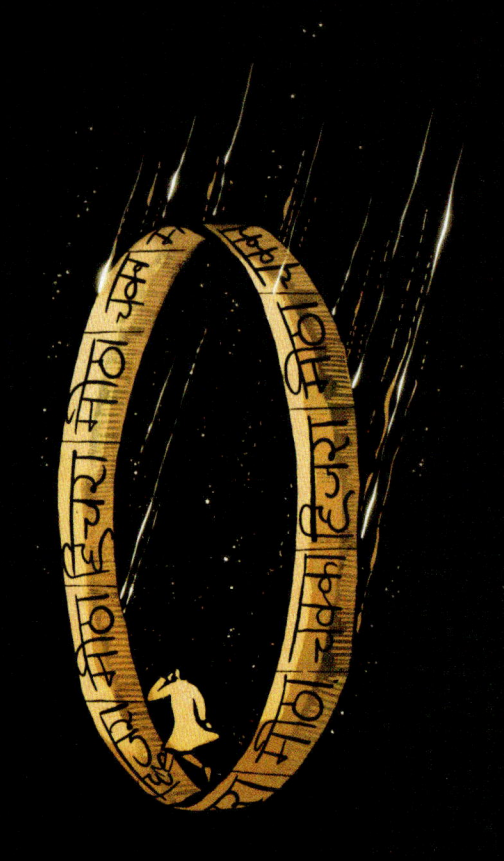

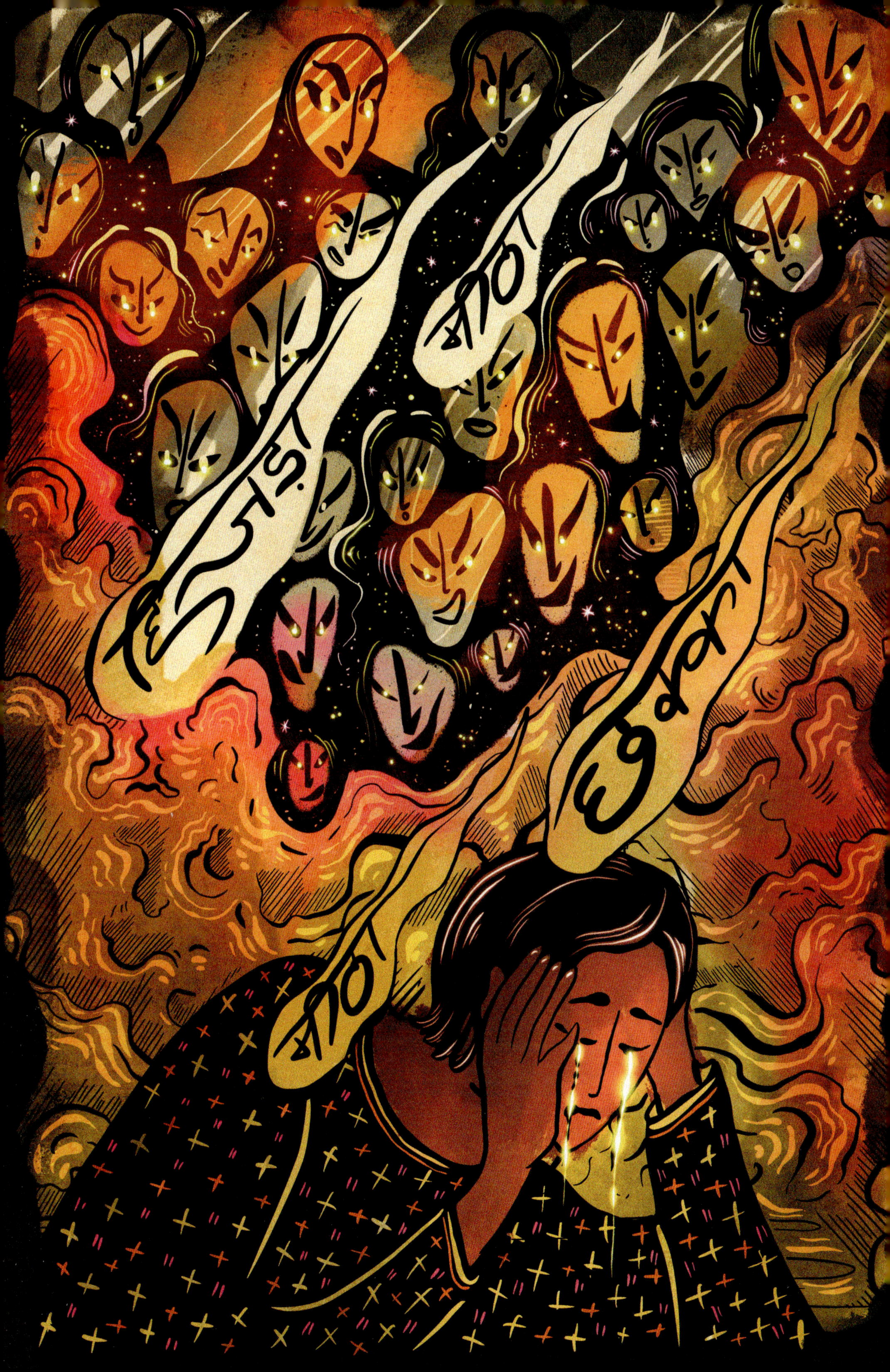
idiot
idiot

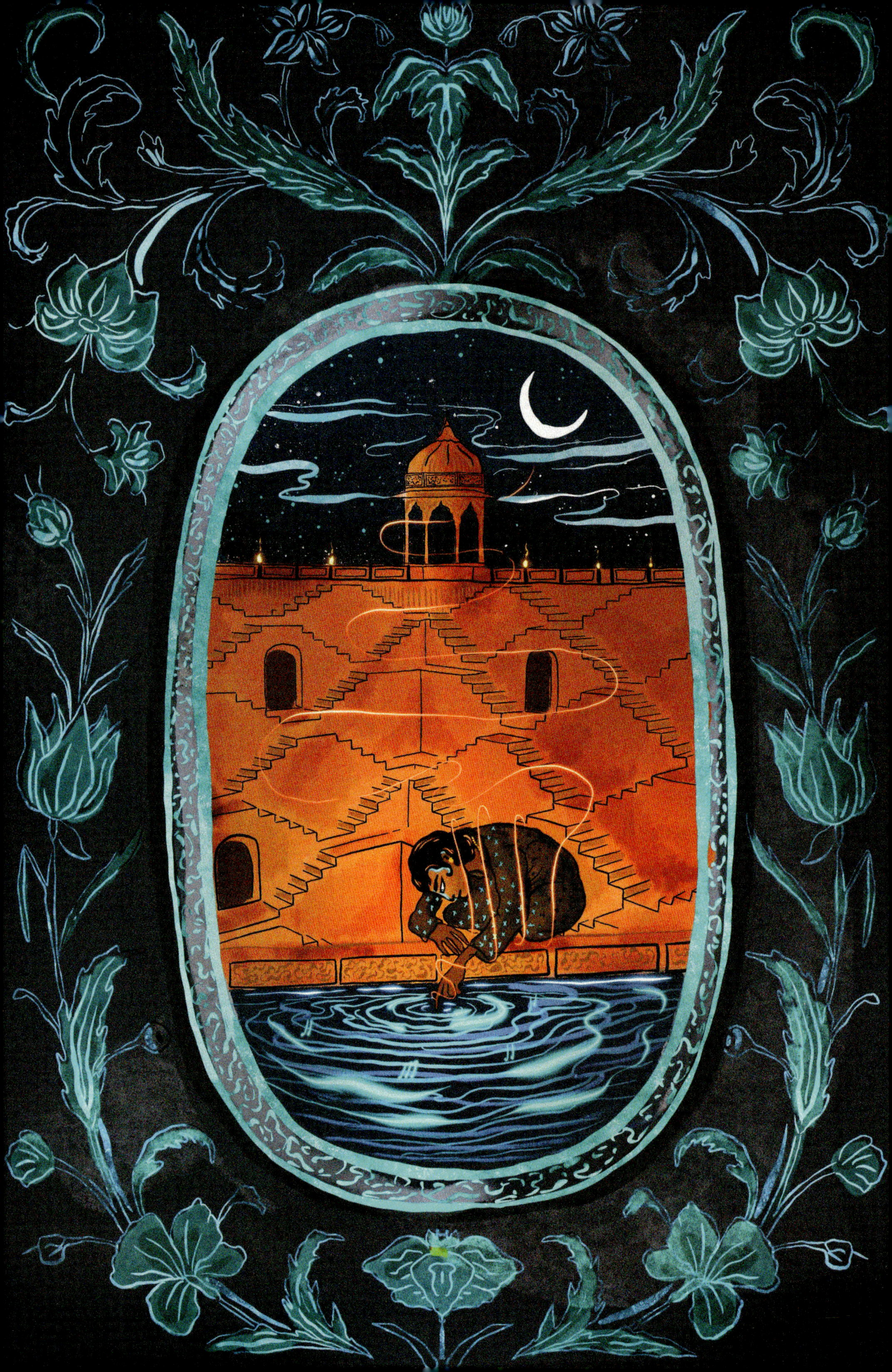

He recalls
the scents
the sounds
the beat
of his heart as he danced.

He feels the cool comfort of coins.
The crinkle of notes.
Money for food and school.
Hope for his sisters.

And
deep down
he clings
to the spark that was lit,
and he wonders,
can he?
Dare he?
Not softly.
Not quietly.
But for all to see.

For two years,
The dancer lives two lives.
Jeers and insults in the day.
Acclaim and applause at night.

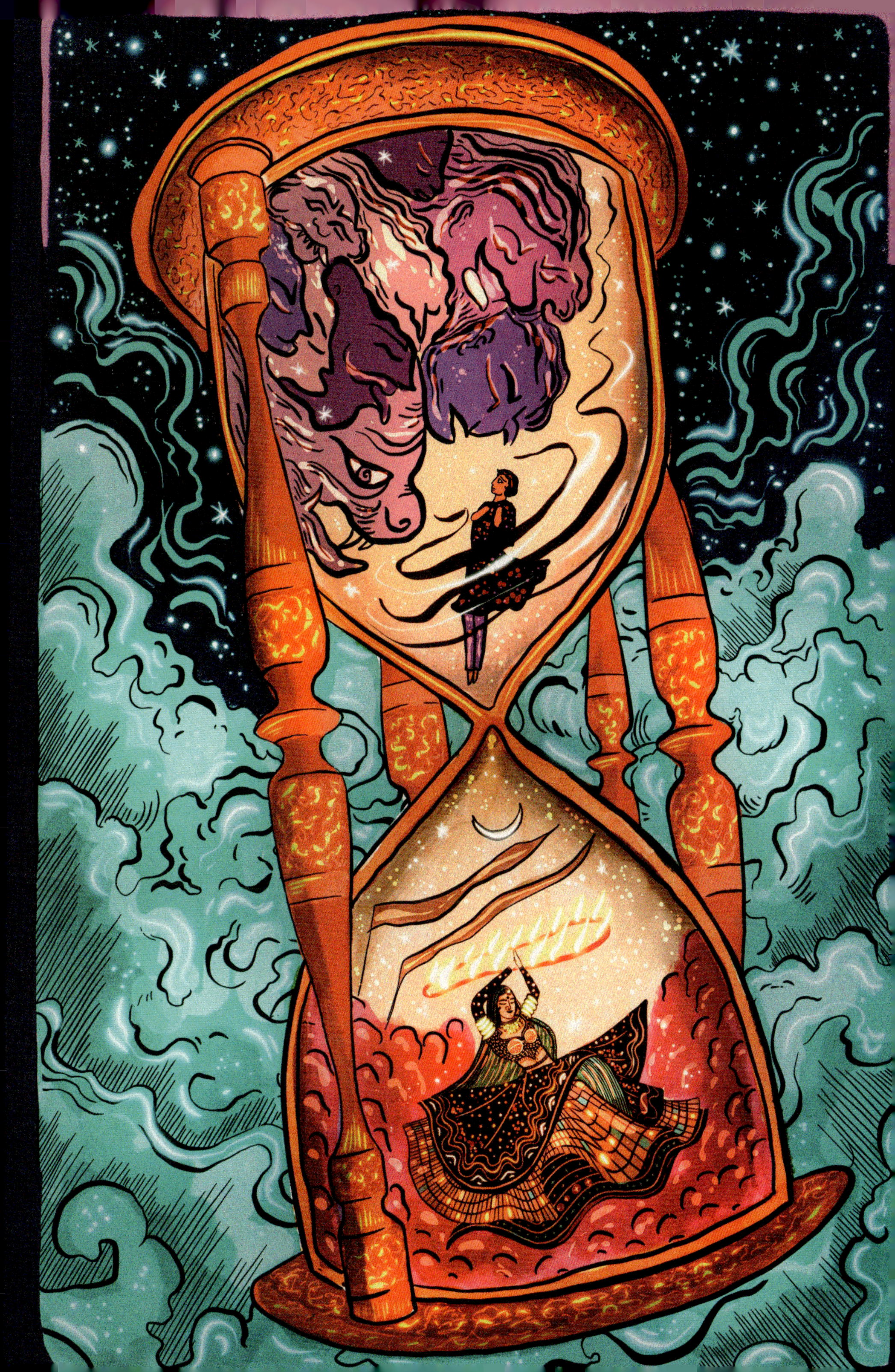

For two years, the dancer studies, trains, rehearses, performs...

Khalbeliya
Bhavai
Ghoomar –
dances steeped
in the history of the desert
and the haunting melodies
of folklore.

She beckons,
welcomes, embraces.
turning hate aside.

And slowly...
oh, so slowly,
the taunts and slurs
fade away...
vanquished by grace and grit.

Word spreads
of the dancer
like a puff of sand borne on the desert wind.

She weaves through her audience,
touching an elder's feet for blessings,
gathering little ones in a giggly embrace,
inviting families to spin and sway with her.

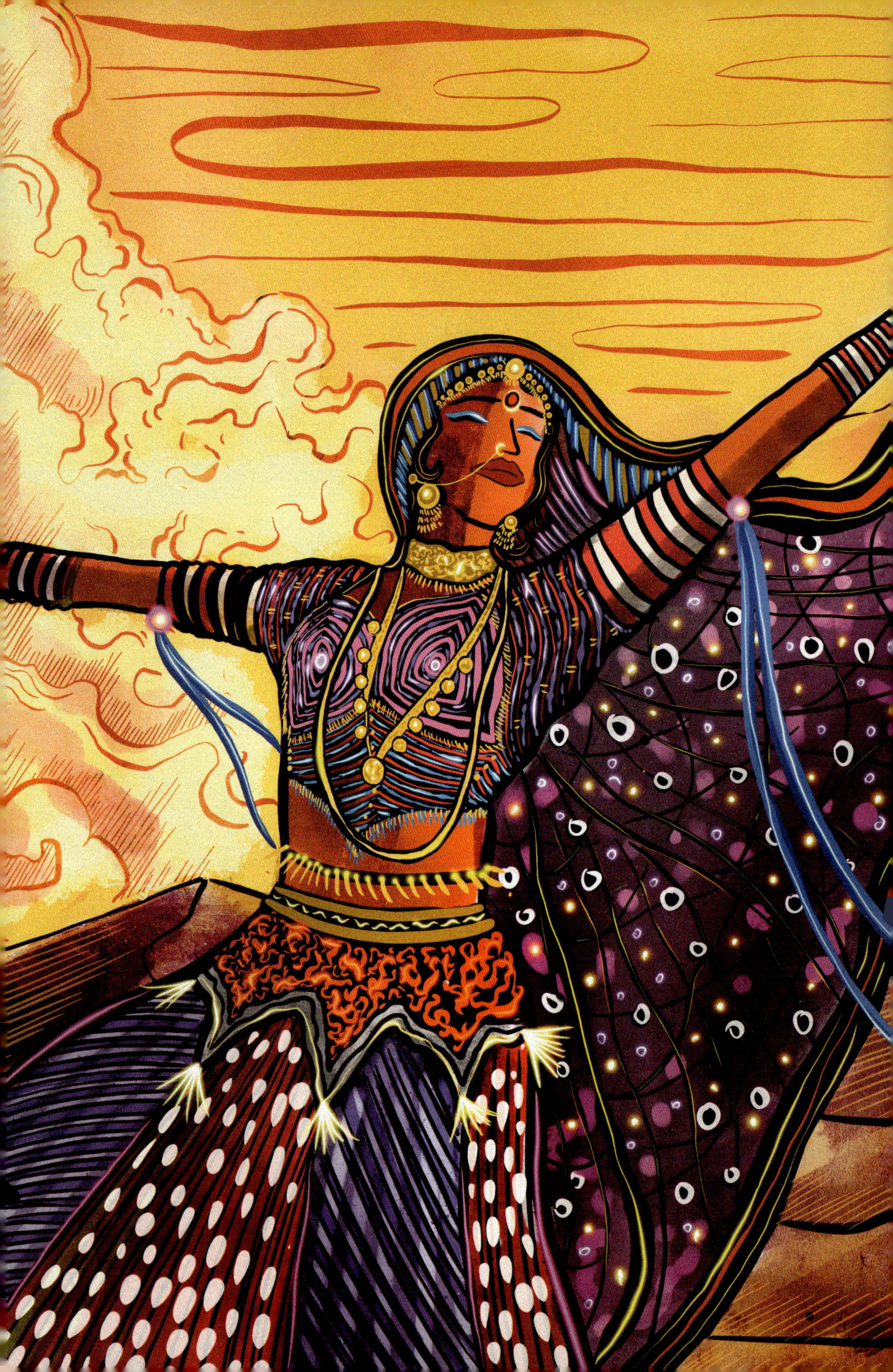

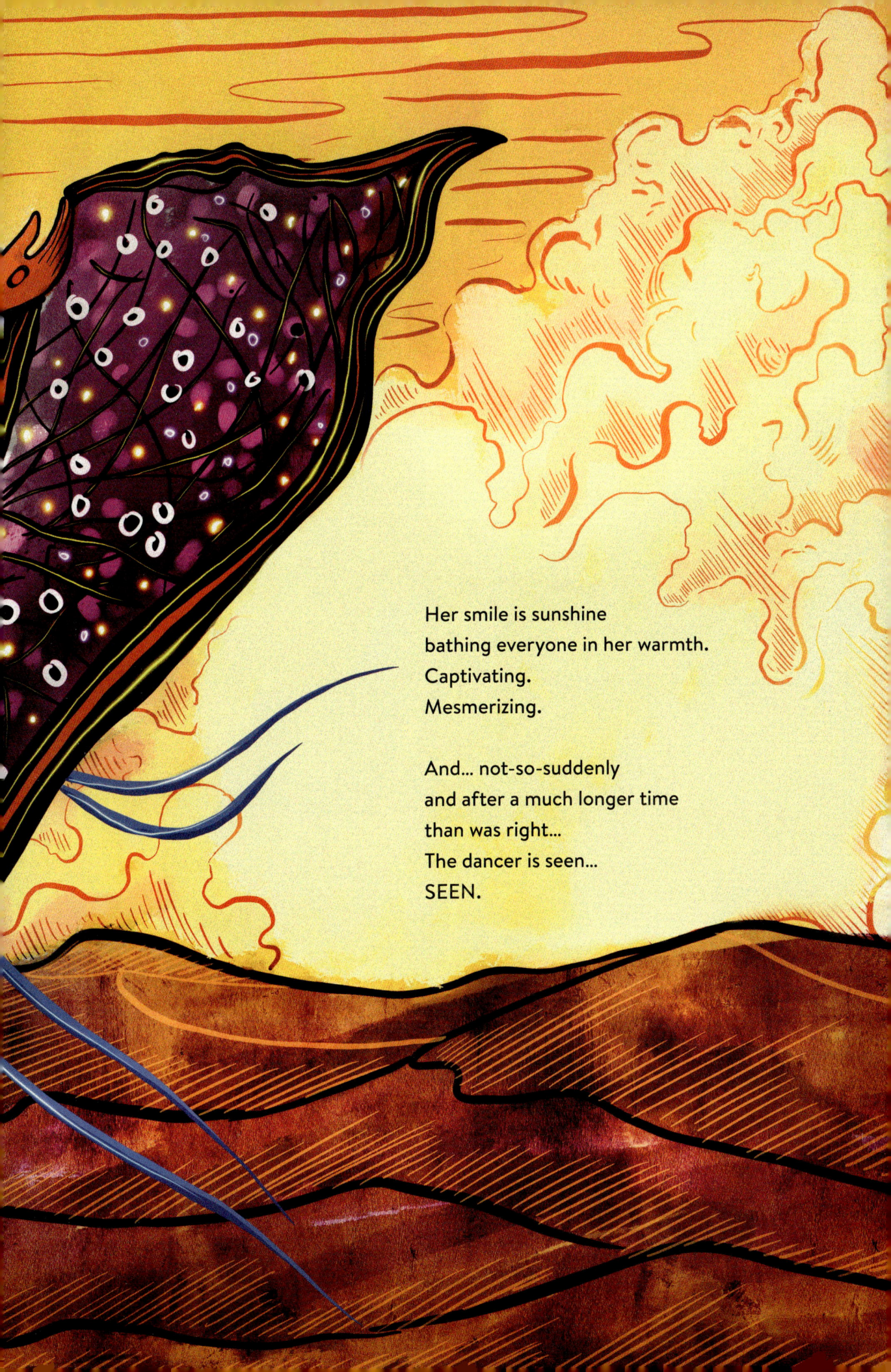

Her smile is sunshine
bathing everyone in her warmth.
Captivating.
Mesmerizing.

And... not-so-suddenly
and after a much longer time
than was right...
The dancer is seen...
SEEN.

Not
Boy OR girl.
Man OR woman.

But
fluid
flowing
like a dance
in between
and all around.

No more hiding.
No more lines in the
sand.

Because
He is She
She is He
and BOTH
are the DESERT QUEEN.

Author's Note

Desert Queen was inspired by drag performer Queen Harish, known as the "Whirling Desert Queen of Rajasthan." I met her at a concert in Rajasthan, India, in the middle of the Thar Desert, where she performed every year. She mesmerized us with her talent, but I was most struck by the compassion, humor, and love that radiated from her when she spoke. She had every single member of the audience, from the youngest to the oldest, captivated. Tragically, Queen Harish was killed in a car accident on her way back from a performance on June 9, 2019. The world lost a bright light. This story is dedicated to her.

About Queen Harish

As a child, Harish Kumar loved watching Bollywood movies and choreographing dances in his head. After school, he would visit the musicians and dance troupes of Jaisalmer to watch them perform. Because of what people thought boys should and shouldn't do, Harish kept his interest in dancing hidden. But when his parents died, young Harish needed a way to support his sisters. He turned to dance.

When he put on the traditional female clothes of a Rajasthani folk dancer, Harish said he felt like the most beautiful person in the world. He loved the smell of make-up and lipstick, the shine and glitter of his costume. In dancing as a woman, Harish found his passion and his vocation. Despite the harsh criticism he faced, Harish trained and performed, developing his own blend of Rajasthani folk and Bollywood dance routines. As his fame grew, dancers from all over came to learn from him. He gave free lessons to young students in his hometown and was a fierce advocate for the folk musicians and artists of Rajasthan. Jaisalmer, where he lived with his wife and two children, grew to embrace their native son, and he became a beloved state and national icon.

Artist's Note

The art for this book was created using pen and ink and then painted with over twenty layers of detail combining color-blocking, detailing, and textures to bring in a vivid color palette. All of the details, patterns, and motifs that appear in the art are rooted in and inspired by Jaisalmer's cultural heritage; that includes miniature paintings, Jain temple architecture, details of Jaisalmer fort, textiles, frescos, and murals of the city.